PHILIP EGLIN

my dad makes
cute ladies
Oliver

For Jennet, Oliver and Morgan

Designed by Philip Eglin and Tony Hayward
© Alison Britton, Philip Eglin and Oliver Watson 1997
Published by Philip Eglin
Printed by Inglis Allen, Kirkcaldy
ISBN 0 9531012 0 7

Published to coincide with an exhibition of new work by Philip Eglin
at The Scottish Gallery, Edinburgh, 7 July – 2 August 1997

Ceramic Traditions

An all-too-small space in the V&A displays some 250 British studio pots from a collection of over 800 pieces by 200 or so studio potters; it is sandwiched between vast historic collections – earthenwares and stonewares back to the medieval period in one direction, porcelains via Chelsea and Meissen to the Chinese in another. Every one of the studio pots inevitably connects back in one way or another – technical or visual – to something in this rich tradition. Yet surprisingly few engage deeply with ceramic's past: most could happily exist quite remote from it. The work of only a special few gains immeasurably in strength and resonance when shown in this historic context. Bernard Leach and Michael Cardew single themselves out immediately, for example, for their pots *look* so much like old things. More surprising are those potters whose work looks like nothing from the past, yet who are just as tightly bound to their "heritage": Richard Slee, for example, is one, and Philip Eglin another.

Of course, there is no real "tradition" that connects studio pottery back to the past – no natural continuance of making according to age-old customs for age-old uses. Studio pottery is an invention of the twentieth century. The nearest thing we come to such an "organic tradition", where the same community has made the same things in the same ways for the same market is surely in Stoke-on-Trent, where blue-printed willow-pattern has been churned out continuously for two centuries. But "tradition" and "industry" are in the popular mind polar opposites.

Bernard Leach understood this in his call for a "reforging" of tradition – an explicit acknowledgement that traditions are mostly, as Eric Hobsbawm puts it, "invented" – designed to "inculcate certain values and norms" and usually stressing a spurious continuity with the past. Leach's work was meaningful only because the "tradition" to which it referred had died. Hobsbawm observes that "...the wigs of lawyers could hardly acquire their modern significance until other people stopped wearing wigs."[1] Equally, Leach's work could not gain meaning until "real" hand-made pottery had perished. Leach's work, and that of his school, literally invents a link with certain parts of the past, and this link can only be ideological.

Eglin reforges "tradition" in another way. He links in the realm of ideas a wide range of past things that may have had only the most subtle "organic" connection. In his ways of making, subject matter, object types and decoration, he makes links between fine art and decorative; between Cranach, Manet and Picasso on one side and Meissen figurines, Staffordshire flatbacks, and willow-pattern wares on the other; between the hand of the artist and the repetitive transfer, the significant mark and the random splash, between inscription and graffiti. He makes no call to a reactionary ideology grounded in the past, rather he re-energises the past, and illuminates it, sending a powerfully directed beam back in time to pick out what he sees as important concerns which are still of value. Here indeed is a "tradition", no less real than any other for being invented, and all the more important for reclaiming the past while steadfastly directing our gaze to the future.

Oliver Watson

[1] E.Hobsbawn, "Introduction", *The Invention of Tradition*, Canto Edition., 1992, pp. 1-4.

Comfort and Surprise.

Philip Eglin has used art history to his own ends in his work and reminds us of familiar objects, making a new kind of domestic and approachable artefact that carries the narrative of other things. When I first wrote an essay about him in 1991[1] his figures were the main achievement. I thought he was succeeding in combining an artist's choosy, tactile feeling for the past – of pre-industrial ceramics and Cranach paintings – with an intuitive and skilful fabrication of things relevant to contemporary interests and desires.

Several years on, he is even better at the figures. They are subtler in pose. Some are now tiny, though larger than a Meissen figurine, and honey glazed or blue and white. The lighter small-scale sharpens the detail; little hands, the tilt of the head. Larger pieces are strange seated women, absorbed and at ease, their skin rich with pigment. He layers patterns and images, collaging diverse drawings: printed, painted, bleeding or controlled. Facility has not polished out the innocence of the figures.

They have been much admired. Some artists in his position would be constrained by the strength of the demand. But for the last few years, interestingly, he has turned to other looser forms as well.

If you are wrapped up in ceramics as I am, it gets harder to be breathtaken by a ceramic object. But I had a moment of vivid surprise when I saw the first of Eglin's 'bucket' pots a couple of years ago. Why was I thrilled? They are not particularly remarkable shapes; slack cylinders, a bit slewed. He needed a change and wanted to make a shape he didn't know about. An 'ordinary' form freed him for serious playing with the surface. In this casual setting, delightful ambiguity sways the understanding of the crowded iconography. His kids' drawings, his own, the Lottery logo, Manet paintings, words, Lego Indians: old and new images. The fit and the unfit, decoratively, fight it out on the pot wall. This is fluent wit with scale and meaning in the round. Eglin's lines have the relaxed vitality of the painting on the backs of plates, or in the border around a serious painting. Cobalt blue, inky but staunchly ceramic, dominates in scratched drawings picked up in slip on the flat clay slabs, or as a pure oxide monoprint transferred on tissue onto the glaze-fired surface. Occasional lines of brash red glaze disturb the blue-and-white convention.

The channel-hopping complexity of images and brushmarks combines the distant and the close. To 'lift' images from elsewhere, even your own son, is to work at one remove from authorship. But he is at the same time using snatches of what's happening in life, which is close like a diary.

The beautiful surfaces he improvised on the buckets recharged, perhaps, his current work with figures. Eglin is an artist who revisits subjects and ideas, plays them again. In making the figures he can have command of brave representational structure, which is tough in clay if you are working hollow like a potter. With the buckets he can have unforeseen shape, the perk of inside/outside, and be a painter.

Alison Britton

---

[1] Exhibition leaflet for 'Philip Eglin: A Staffordshire Tradition?', South Bank Centre, London 1991

1. Venus Plate 1989

2. Le Déjeuner sur l'Herbe Plate 1989

3. Madonna col Bambino 1992

4. Bucket 1995

5. Venus et Amour 1995

6. Reclining Nude 1995

7. Seated Nude 1996

8. Reclining Nude 1996

9. Seated Nude 1996

10. Where's Mrs Andrews? 1996

11. Venus et Amour 1997

12. Reclining Nude 1997

13. Seated Nude 1997

14. Seated Nude 1997

1. Venus Plate 1989
   diam. 20 cms
   Collection: The Artist

2. Le Déjeuner sur l'Herbe Plate 1989
   diam. 20 cms
   Private Collection: Leicester

3. Madonna col Bambino 1992
   73 x 28 x 36 cms
   Fitzwilliam Museum, Cambridge

4. Bucket 1995
   ht. 45 cms
   Collection: The Artist

5. Venus et Amour 1995
   33 x 20 x 13 cms
   Private Collection: Chicago, USA

6. Reclining Nude 1995
   20 x 13 x 33 cms
   Private Collection: New York, USA

7. Seated Nude 1996
   69 x 43 x 26 cms
   Castle Museum, Norwich

8. Reclining Nude 1996
   60 x 24 x 37 cms
   Private Collection: Munich, Germany

9. Seated Nude 1996
   70 x 38 x 26 cms
   Private Collection: York

10. Where's Mrs Andrews? 1996
    ht. 44 cms

11. Venus et Amour 1997
    46 x 20 x 12 cms

12. Reclining Nude 1997
    32 x 12 x 18 cms

13. Seated Nude 1997
    61 x 38 x 28 cms

14. Seated Nude 1997
    38 x 21 x 17 cms

Work in Public Collections include Allen Gallery, Alton
Aukland Museum, New Zealand   Castle Museum, Norwich
City Museum, Stoke-on-Trent   Victoria & Albert Museum, London
Fitzwilliam Museum, Cambridge   Portsmouth Museum and Art Gallery
Liverpool Museum and Art Gallery   Hove Museum and Art Gallery
Shipley Museum and Art Gallery, Gateshead   Crafts Council, London

Born 1959 Gibraltar

1979-82   Staffordshire Polytechnic, Stoke-on-Trent
1983-86   Royal College of Art, London

1991   Crafts Council Selected Index
1993   Arts Foundation Fellowship
1996   Jerwood Prize for Applied Arts: Ceramics

Solo Exhibitions

1990   Stafford Art Gallery, Stafford
1991   Oxford Gallery, Oxford
        Philip Eglin – A Staffordshire Tradition?
        The South Bank Centre, London
1993   Crafts Council Shop, Victoria & Albert Museum, London
1994   The Scottish Gallery, Edinburgh
1995   Garth Clark Gallery, New York, USA
1997   The Scottish Gallery, Edinburgh

Selected Group Exhibitions

1989   Clay Bodies
        Contemporary Applied Arts, London
1990   The Decade Ahead
        The Scottish Gallery, Edinburgh
1991   The Abstract Vessel
        Oriel, Cardiff
        Aspects of Sculpture
        Galerie fur Englische Keramic, Sandhausen, Germany
        Favourite Things
        Crafts Council Gallery, London
        Beyond the Dovetail
        Crafts Council Gallery, London
        Colours of the Earth – Twentieth Century British Ceramics
        British Council Touring Exhibition, India
1992   25th Anniversary Exhibition
        Contemporary Applied Arts, London
1993   The Raw and the Cooked
        Museum of Modern Art, Oxford (touring exhibition)
1995   One from the Heart
        Aberystwth Arts Centre, Dyfed (touring exhibition)
        The Nude in Clay
        Perimeter Gallery, Chicago, USA
1996   Hot off the Press
        Tullie House, Carlisle (touring exhibition)
        10 Years Crafts
        The Scottish Gallery, Edinburgh
        Jerwood Prize Exhibition
        Crafts Council Gallery, London (touring exhibition)
1996   Philip Eglin and Claire Curneen
        Contemporary Applied Arts, London
        Objects of Our Time
        Crafts Council Gallery, London (touring exhibition)

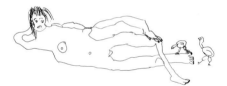

Frontispiece and tailpiece drawings by Oliver Eglin